# Gladys Aylward
# 1902–1970

## Sydney Wood

Sydney Wood has written numerous history books for primary and secondary schools, as well as books and articles for adults. He is a former senior lecturer in history and is actively involved in curriculum development.

Picture credits

Hulton Deutsch Collection/Corbis: page 6
Wolfgang Kaehler/Corbis: page 11
Popperfoto: page 19
Camera Press: page 20
Ronald Grant Archive: page 21

Published by 4Learning

124 Horseferry Road
London
SW1P 2TX

©2001 Channel Four Television Corporation

Written by Sydney Wood
Edited by Anne Fleck and Jackie Mace
Illustrated by Gary Wing
Picture research by ilumi
Designed by HA Design
Printed by ESP Colour
ISBN 186215 8606

For further information about 4Learning and
details of published materials, e-mail
4learning.info@channel4.co.uk
www.channel4.com/learning

# Contents

Gladys sets off ............................................. 4

A very difficult journey ............................. 6

Living with Jeannie .................................... 8

Gladys meets the Mandarin ................... 10

Gladys goes to prison ........................... 12

Gladys has to leave Yangcheng ...... 14

The journey to the Yellow River ..... 16

The great journey continues ............ 18

Gladys Aylward's later years ........... 20

A timeline of Gladys' life .................. 22

Index ............................................................. 24

More books to read ............................. 24

# Gladys sets off

Gladys Aylward was born in London in 1902. When she left school Gladys became a servant. She worked for rich people, cleaning, dusting, lighting fires and serving meals. But Gladys wanted a different life. She believed God wanted her to go to China to persuade people there to become Christians, so in 1930, she went to a college to train for this.

I'm afraid you must leave Miss Aylward. You haven't done very well. And you're too old to learn Chinese.

Oh dear! I have no money. I'll have to be a servant again. But I will get to China somehow.

Gladys wrote to a woman called Jeannie Lawson who lived in China. She had heard she needed help. Jeannie wrote back to say she'd be glad to see Gladys – if Gladys could get to China.

It cost £47.50 to travel to China by boat and train. That was a lot of money in those days. It took Gladys many months to save so much. She only had just over £2 left when she'd paid for her tickets. But still she set off, even though there was a war going on between China and Russia at that time.

Goodbye. I'll write to you from China. Don't worry. God will look after me.

# A very difficult journey

Gladys took two suitcases with her. One was full of clothes and the other was full of tins and packets of food. She also took a pan, a kettle and a little stove on which to cook.

The train from London took her to the coast. There, she got on a ship which took her to Holland and then she got on a train which took her to Moscow, in Russia. She made her own meals on the way.

Gladys Aylward left London by train.

In Moscow she got on another train which took her a long way. It stopped because, further ahead, Russian and Chinese soldiers were fighting each other. Gladys had to walk back several miles during the night through snow to the town of Chita. There she got another train to the Russian coast.

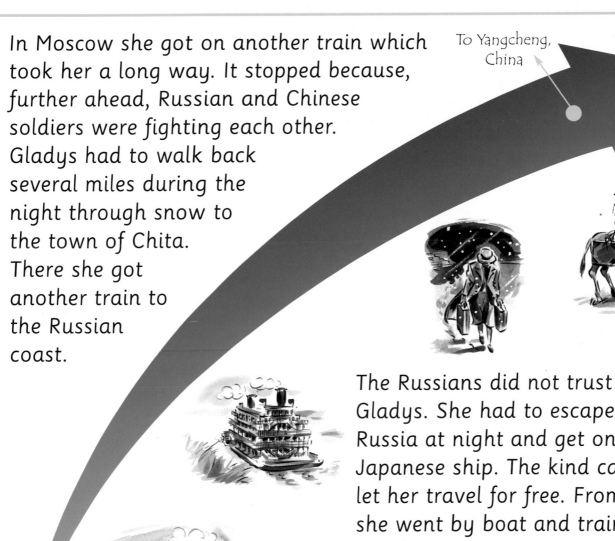

To Yangcheng, China

From London

The Russians did not trust Gladys. She had to escape from Russia at night and get on a Japanese ship. The kind captain let her travel for free. From Japan, she went by boat and train to China. Finally, she had to ride on a mule for two days to reach the little town of Yangcheng which was high up in the mountains. It was to be her new home.

# Living with Jeannie

Mrs Jeannie Lawson was an old lady, but she was very fierce, too. Gladys found local people were not friendly. They even threw mud at her. She could not see how she was ever going to persuade them to become Christians.

Foreign devil! Go away!

Jeannie and Gladys decided to turn their home into an inn. Many travellers passed through the town. Most of them carried the things they sold on mules. Muleteers are people who drive mules. Jeannie hoped that she and Gladys would be able to tell those muleteers about Christianity.

THE INN OF EIGHT HAPPINESSESS

Good food! Good beds! No fleas here! Come in and we'll tell you stories!

At first the muleteers walked past. So Gladys began grabbing the mules and dragging them in. The muleteers found there was very good food at the inn. It was cooked by Yang, Jeannie's cook. Once they had eaten, they wanted to hear the stories they'd been promised.

# Gladys meets the Mandarin

Gladys was just getting used to her life when Jeannie died. Now she only had Yang the cook to help her. One day he rushed in to tell her she had to meet the Mandarin. The Mandarin was in charge of the area. He had the power to put people in prison. He could even give the order to have their heads chopped off. Now he had a job for Gladys.

You are now my Inspector of Women's Feet. I will pay you. Go to all the nearby villages. I will send soldiers with you.

Chinese baby girls had cloth tied tightly round their feet for many years. This was to stop their feet growing because small feet were supposed to be beautiful. But it meant they could not walk properly. Now the government wanted this habit to end. Gladys visited mountain villages to carry out this order. While she was there she told the people about Christianity.

The Mandarin orders you to free your feet. And then I'm going to tell you stories about Jesus.

A Chinese woman with cloth tied round her feet.

# Gladys goes to prison

**G**ladys' work made her quite important. Local people were no longer against her. One day a messenger ran into the inn yard. He had come from the Mandarin. He shouted for Gladys. He seemed very worried.

You must come to prison at once! The Mandarin needs you.

You must go in. You must stop the fighting. Your God will protect you.

The prisoners were fighting.
One of them had a big axe.
The Mandarin, the Prison Governor and
the guards did not dare go into the prison.

Gladys went into the prison. She stood alone. She was a very small person. The prisoners were all men and many of them were fighting. The prisoner with the axe ran up to Gladys. She spoke loudly to him.

Stop all this fighting. Give me the axe.

Amazingly, the fighting stopped. The prisoner gave Gladys his axe. The guards came back in. The Mandarin and the Governor were delighted. Gladys began to go to the prison every week. She found ways of getting work for the prisoners. She told them stories about Jesus and some prisoners became Christians. Some earned enough money to be able to leave the prison. Gladys even managed to persuade the Governor to let out the prisoners for a day. They came to the inn to hear a talk about Christianity.

# The journey to the Yellow River

Gladys and nearly 100 children set off to walk to Sian, the place of safety. Some children were only five years old. The Mandarin sent two of his men with them for the first three days. They carried sacks of grain. Gladys carried a big cooking pot. In the evening she boiled the grain to make a meal.

But the Mandarin's men had to go back to their homes. The food was soon eaten. Then Gladys and the children met Chinese soldiers who gave them more food. One night they slept in a church that was full of rats. On other nights they slept in the open air among rocks.

For 12 days the children scrambled over the mountains. The path was often very steep and narrow. The children's sandals wore out and they were very hungry. Many cried. Gladys, too, was hungry and tired. She was also ill.

What shall we do now? Please help us, God.

They reached the Yellow River. It was very wide and they could not see any boats. The only person that they met was a very old man who told them that the Japanese were coming.

# The great journey continues

For three days Gladys and the children waited, tired and hungry. Then Chinese soldiers appeared. They had a boat. It was dangerous to cross the river because Japanese aeroplanes often attacked boats, but the trip was managed safely. Gladys and the children walked on. At the next town they heard they could catch a train. The children were excited. They had never seen a train before. Then the train arrived.

It's a dragon! Run!

It's a monster!

The children had to be calmed down. For four days they travelled by train. Then the Japanese bombed the railway. Once more the children walked wearily through the mountains. After four more days they reached the town of Tung Kwan. The only train from there carried coal, not people. Gladys placed her children among the lumps of coal.

Gladys found the journey to Sian difficult.

When they got off the coal train, there was yet another train to catch. Finally they reached Sian. Now they would be safe. But the town gates were shut. 'The town is full,' called a guard. 'You can't come in.' After another weary journey, they reached the town of Fufeng. Here the children were welcomed. They were washed and given food and clothes. But by now Gladys was so ill she could not even stand up.

**G**ladys was taken to hospital in a cart. She was very ill for many months.

> Poor woman. She is so weak she may very well die.

Gladys is remembered for leading children to safety.

Gladys got better and went back to work. But there did not seem to be anywhere safe to live. The Japanese were finally defeated, but the Chinese were now fighting each other. The Chinese side that finally won this war – the Communists – hated Christians like Gladys.

After many years in China, Gladys longed to see her family in London. Kind Americans paid for her to fly home. She worked for Chinese people who had lived in England for several years, but she still wanted to go back to China. Many of Gladys' friends now lived on the island of Taiwan, near the Chinese coast. She set off to join them and continued to help poor children.

A scene from a film about Gladys.

Gladys died in 1970. By then, books had been written about her and a very successful film of her life had been made. The story of her amazing bravery and her strong religious beliefs will long be remembered.

# A timeline of Gladys' life

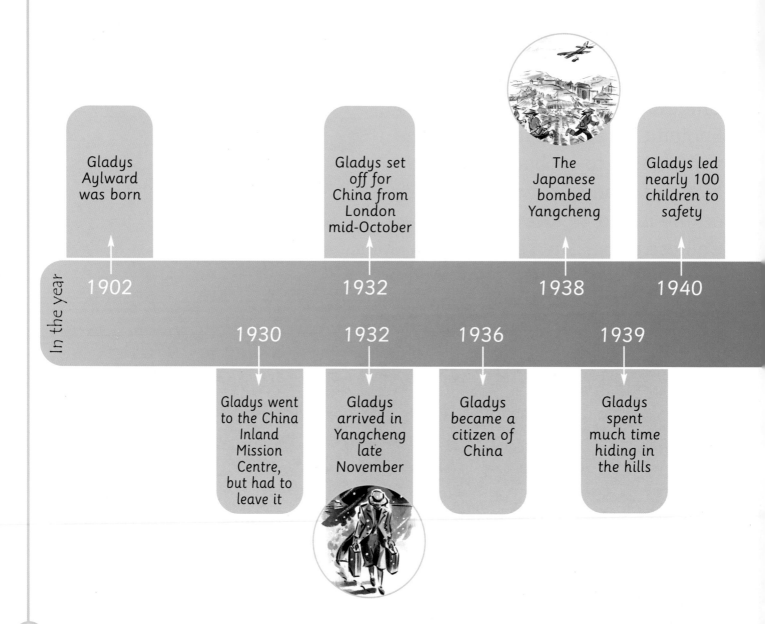

In the year

**1902** — Gladys Aylward was born

**1930** — Gladys went to the China Inland Mission Centre, but had to leave it

**1932** — Gladys set off for China from London mid-October

**1932** — Gladys arrived in Yangcheng late November

**1936** — Gladys became a citizen of China

**1938** — The Japanese bombed Yangcheng

**1939** — Gladys spent much time hiding in the hills

**1940** — Gladys led nearly 100 children to safety

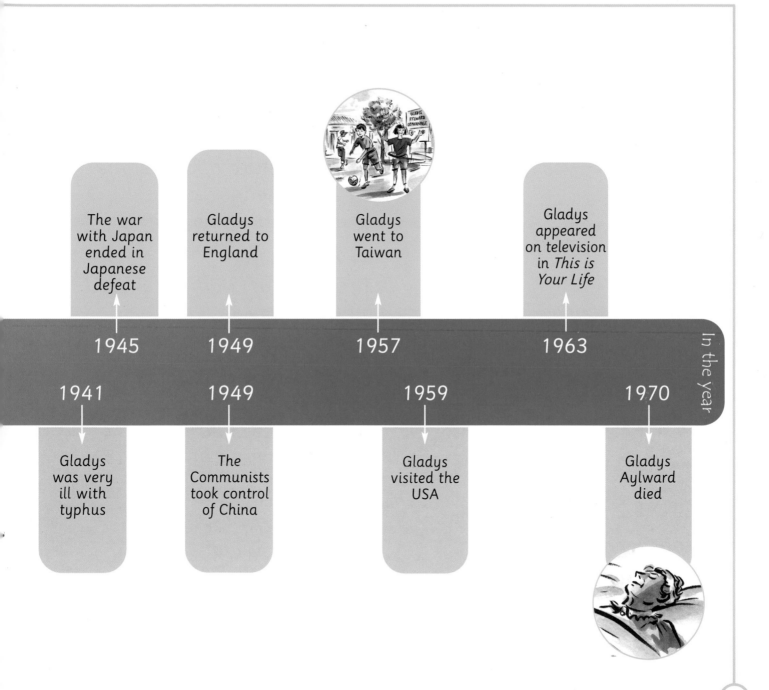

The war with Japan ended in Japanese defeat

**1945**

Gladys returned to England

**1949**

Gladys went to Taiwan

**1957**

Gladys appeared on television in *This is Your Life*

**1963**

**1941**

Gladys was very ill with typhus

**1949**

The Communists took control of China

**1959**

Gladys visited the USA

**1970**

Gladys Aylward died

# Index

Ai-weh-deh; 14

Christianity; 9, 11, 13

Communists; 20

Fufeng; 19

Inspector of Women's
Feet; 10

Lawson, Jeannie; 5, 8–10

Mandarin; 10–13, 16

Ninepence; 14

Prison; 10, 12–13

Sian; 16, 19

Taiwan; 21

Yangcheng; 7, 14–15

Yellow River; 17

## More books to read

*Gladys Aylward:
The Adventure of a Lifetime*
by Janet Benge
(Ywam Publishing, 1998)

*Never Say Die:
The Story of Gladys Aylward*
by Cyril Davey
(Lutterworth, 1986 edition)

*Gladys Aylward:
The Little Woman*
by Christine Hunter
(Moody Press, 1981)

*Gladys Aylward:
Missionary in China*
by Sam Wellman
(Barbour & Co, 1998)